The Adventures of Nacho & Nellie in New Orleans

Copyright © 2024 by Kathryn Bond & Mary Lovell

All rights reserved.

No part of this publication may be reproduced, distributed, or transmitted in any form or by any means, including photocopying, recording, or other electronic or mechanical methods, without the prior written permission of the publisher, except as permitted by U.S. copyright law.

Book Cover by Kathryn Bond

Illustrations by Kathryn Bond

To our Family,

Thank you for always believing
in us and encouraging us to follow our dreams.

"Nacho, wait up! Are you sure we should be running off to Nola?", Nellie nervously asks.
"Come on Nellie, it's the Big Easy,
you will surely have a blast!"

They enter the city with their heads held high.
There are so many places for them to explore and try.

They stop short in their tracks when they smell
a breakfast oh-so-fond;
sweet beignets from Cafe Du Monde!

They sip their coffee and devour their share,
while loads of powdered sugar fly everywhere!

With traces of sugar still in their hair,
Nacho and Nellie move on to the French Quarter
without the smallest care.

The streets are buzzing with artist and musicians galore.
There are so many places for them to explore!

After the French Quarter,
Nacho and Nellie want to see another view.
Where better than a trip to the Audubon Zoo?

Nellie says, "I can't wait to see other cats and
dogs while we walk around."
But at this zoo, that is not what they found.

Lions and tigers and bears, oh my!
Nacho and Nellie sprint from the zoo
without even saying goodbye.

They ran straight towards the Superdome,
without so much as a yield.
Next thing you know, they're on the football field!

Fans are cheering "Go Saints!" and "Who Dat!".
Nellie mishears them and thinks they are
cheering for Nacho the cat.

The two are starstruck and on quite the roll.
Before you know it, they're racing towards the field goal.

After all the excitement, they realize they forgot to eat lunch.
As their tummies grumble, they need to find
food fast. They're in quite the crunch.

Suddenly a smell of Cajun spices fills the air.
Nellie sniffs out a local crawfish boil just beyond the square.

The two feast on all the fixins - crawfish, corn, potatoes, and more.
With their bellies all full, they are ready for what is next in-store.

As they leave the boil, Nacho and Nellie find reason to be afraid.
A large crowd is forming for a Mardi Gras parade!

The masks and throws scare them at first,
but then they see all sorts of fun stuff,
including a giant confetti burst.

They quickly realize there are free beads and toys galore.
They make their way to the front of the
crowd to catch some more.

After catching more than they can carry,
the two friends stumble upon City Park, all green and airy.

Nellie goes wild when he sees a majestic swan.
He runs across the bridge so he can gaze on.

Nacho and Nellie take their time walking around.
What other wonderful sites could be found?

Nellie says, "Wow, I didn't realize that
New Orleans was so much fun!"
"Our adventure is not over yet," Nacho purs.
"There is one more thing to be done."

To wrap up their trip and make it complete,
Nacho and Nellie make a pit stop for a sweet treat.

NOLA sno-balls are the perfect snack.
They enjoy their treats as they finally head back.

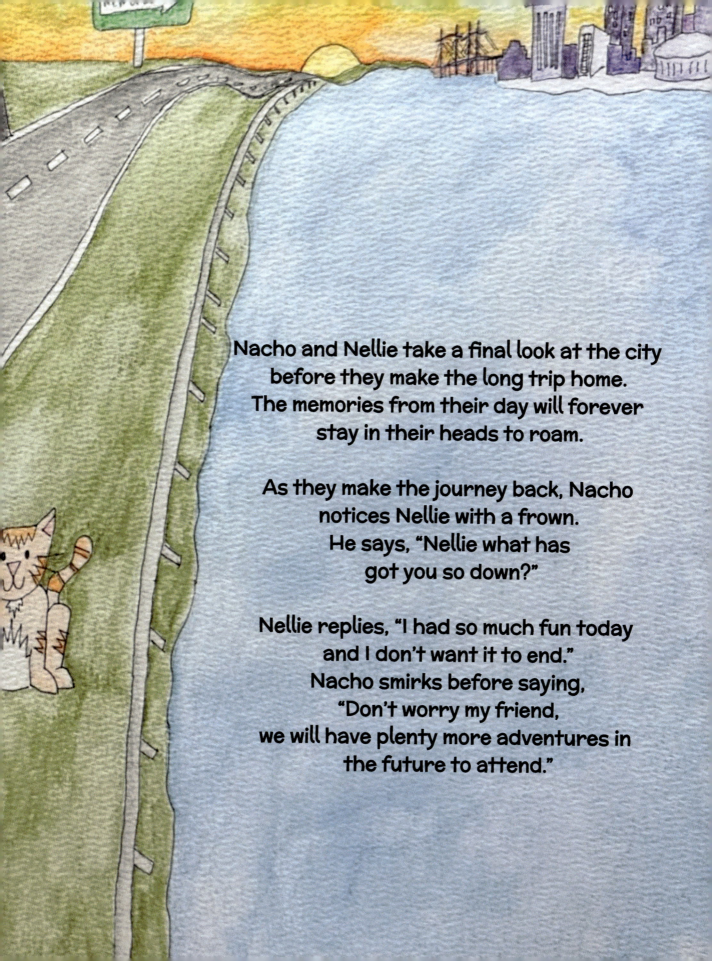

Nacho and Nellie take a final look at the city
before they make the long trip home.
The memories from their day will forever
stay in their heads to roam.

As they make the journey back, Nacho
notices Nellie with a frown.
He says, "Nellie what has
got you so down?"

Nellie replies, "I had so much fun today
and I don't want it to end."
Nacho smirks before saying,
"Don't worry my friend,
we will have plenty more adventures in
the future to attend."

Meet the Real Nacho & Nellie

NACHO

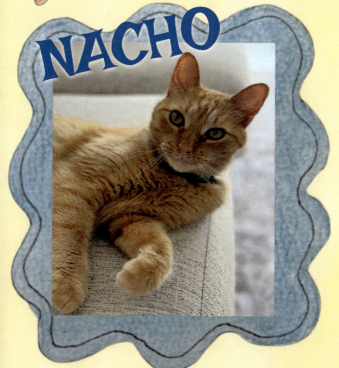

Meet Nacho. He might look like your ordinary household cat, but he is much more than that! Nacho is an orange Tabby cat who is currently 8 years old. He lives on the Mississippi Gulf Coast with his owners, Kathryn and Jake. He enjoys roaming the outdoors, playing with boxes, and taking naps in his free time.

Meet Nellie. His smile says it all – he's quite the charmer, but don't let that fool you, he can get into some trouble when he's tempted. Nellie is 4 years old and lives with his mom Mary, on the Northshore in Louisiana. He loves car rides, playing fetch, shopping trips, and most of all, chicken!

NELLIE

Want to see more of Nacho & Nellie? Check them out on Instagram!

@_nachoordinarycat   @nelliethecavapooo

Made in the USA
Monee, IL
19 December 2024